FAR OUT
FAIRY TALES

INTRODUCING...

ALFRED THE SWORDMAKER

THE DRAGON

THE VILLAGE KNIGHTS

in...

Raintree is an imprint of Capstone Global
Library Limited, a company incorporated
in England and Wales having its registered
office at 264 Banbury Road, Oxford,
OX2 7DY – Registered company number:
6695582

www.raintree.co.uk
myorders@raintree.co.uk

Designed by Hilary Wacholz
Edited by Mandy Robbins
Printed and bound in the UK.

978 1 3982 04911

British Library Cataloguing in Publica
Data
A full catalogue record for this boc
available from the British Library

FAR OUT FAIRY TALES

THE DRAGON AND THE SWORDMAKER

A GRAPHIC NOVEL

BY STEPHANIE PETERS

ILLUSTRATED BY FERN CANO

As the years went by, the dragons disappeared.

So did the knights in need of the sharpest swords in the land.

Can I help you, sir?

No, thank you. I'm fine.

One day, Alfred realized he hadn't made a new sword for months.

Well, that's it, then. Time to lock up . . . for good.

But as he was heading home –

Maybe now I can travel. I will miss making swords, though . . .

SCREEEE!

Is that a . . . dragon?

Ahh! We're doomed!

Alfred knew he should be scared. Dragons were fearsome creatures, after all.

When the knights hear about the dragon, they'll return to the village.

But he wasn't scared. He was excited.

They'll need swords. And that means —

Oof!

But the next morning, Alfred made a startling discovery.

What in the world?

It was the most beautiful sword he'd ever laid eyes on.

Where did it come from?

Did I make it in my sleep?

But he knew that was nonsense.

Everything is just where I left it, and the forge is stone cold!

I've never seen a jewel like this before!

The gem wasn't the only unusual thing about the sword - it glowed!

Ahh!

But when he opened the shop in the morning, he didn't find another sword.

He found two!

What?
How?
Who?

And the morning after that . . .

Three?!

No, just one, please!

Alfred could no longer contain his curiosity.

So that night, he hid inside the shop and waited to see what would happen.

Time dragged on . . .

Then suddenly . . .

RUSTLE RUSTLE

It's coming from the forge!

It will destroy my shop!

And then it will come after me!

Alfred was terrified.

But the dragon surprised him.

What's it doing?

FOOSH!

CLANK!

WHOOSH! WHOOSH!

That's one way to cool the metal.

Amazing!

SCRTCH! SCRTCH! SCRTCH!

CLINK!

See?
I'm totally
fine!

But why
didn't the sword
hurt you?

The dragon told Alfred her story.

So that night, I sneaked down to your shop to blast those swords with my fire breath.

Whoops! That'll leave a mark!

But I couldn't even finish one sword.

But you would have. And that would have meant trouble for me.

I could have waited, then fire-blasted the swords when they were finished.

But it seemed easier to just make them myself.

I can do this!

Because it was the only way I knew I'd be safe.

Alfred was touched by the dragon's story . . . and sad for the part he had played in it.

Is there anything I can do to make up for it?

Actually, there is!

That night, Alfred and the dragon worked side-by-side.

And you're sure you'll be safe from these blades?

FOOSH!

Positive!

The next day, the knights set off for the mountain with their brand-new swords.

Never fear, I'll slay that beast!

Better hurry or those others will slay it first!

None of the knights ever found the dragon, though.

Taste my blade, foul creature!

Save your strength. It's not here.

Huh . . . maybe there's a princess who needs rescuing?

Let's go!

"The Elves and the Shoemaker" was first published in 1812 as part of a collection of fairy tales by Jakob and Wilhelm Grimm - better known as the Brothers Grimm. Since then, it has been retold many times.

In most versions of the original story, an old shoemaker is almost out of leather and money. Without leather, he can't make shoes, and without shoes to sell, he can't pay his rent or buy food. The shoemaker is about to despair. Luckily, some kind-hearted elves sneak into his shop one night and use the leather to make a beautiful pair of shoes. The shoemaker is shocked to find the shoes the next morning. He has no idea who made them, but he is very grateful to the mystery shoemakers. He sells the pair and buys more material. The clever elves turn it into more shoes. This goes on night after night. Finally, the shoemaker decides he must know who his secret helpers are. He hides in his shop. When the elves arrive, he watches them work from his hiding place. Amazed and grateful, he uses leftover scraps of material to make little outfits for them - including shoes, of course!

In some versions, the delighted elves continue to make shoes for the shoemaker. In others, they go on their way, happy to have helped him through a tough time. The shoemaker has a wife in some of the versions too, and she's the one who insists they discover who their helpers are. All versions end happily, with the shoemaker earning enough money to live happily ever after.

A FAR OUT GUIDE TO THE FAIRY TALE'S TWISTS!

The old man in this story doesn't make shoes – he makes swords.

Instead of a group of elves, the secret helper is a friendly dragon.

The elves' shoes don't have magic powers, but the dragon's swords do.

The elves and the shoemaker never work together, but the dragon and the swordmaker do.

VISUAL QUESTIONS

Graphic novels have special ways to show when characters are speaking and when they are thinking. How can you tell when the swordmaker is thinking and when he is speaking?

Is it magic?

How did it get in my shop?

Who made it?

Ho, there, swordmaker! Open up!

Coming!

1

2

Still, if I can't make even one sword . . .

. . . how am I going to make them all?

How do you think the dragon knew that the swordmaker needed help? (Look at page 15 if you need help.)

Sometimes stories change when they get passed on by word of mouth. The art on page 12 shows that happening. Do you think the dragons were ever a threat to the people? Why or why not?

A sound effect, or SFX for short, helps to show and describe sound in comics. What do the SFX show here? How else do you know what's happening?

AUTHOR

Stephanie True Peters has been writing books for young readers for more than 25 years. Among her most recent titles are for Raintree's Far-out Fairy Tale/Folk Tale series. An avid reader, fitness enthusiast and beach wanderer, Stephanie enjoys spending time with her children, Jackson and Chloe, her husband, Dan, and the family's two cats and two rabbits.

ILLUSTRATOR

Fern Cano is an illustrator and colourist who was born in Mexico City, Mexico. He has done work for Marvel, DC Comics and role-playing games like *Pathfinder*. In his spare time, he enjoys hanging out with friends, singing, rowing and drawing!

GLOSSARY

carriage vehicle with wheels that is usually pulled by horses

forge special furnace in which metal is heated

hilt handle of a sword or dagger

knight warrior of the Middle Ages (AD 400–1500) who wore armour and usually fought on horseback

pierce pass through with a sharp instrument

predict say what you think will happen in the future

slay kill in a violent way

talon long, sharp claw

AWESOMELY EVER AFTER.

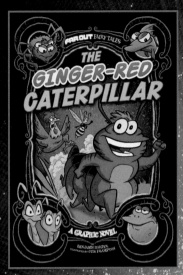

FAR OUT FAIRY TALES

ONLY FROM RAINTREE!